WALKING WITH
WILLIAM OF NORMANDY

STATUE OF WILLIAM THE CONQUEROR, FALAISE, NORMANDY

[Yogananda] told us that, in a former incarnation, he had been William the Conqueror.

—*Conversations with Yogananda* by Swami Kriyananda, p. 189.

WALKING WITH
WILLIAM OF NORMANDY

A Paramhansa Yogananda Pilgrimage Guide

Richard Salva

"March with God. March with God.
Sword in hand, heart afire!"
–Haridas Blake

crystal clarity **publishers**
nevada city, california

Crystal Clarity Publishers • Nevada City, CA 95959
Copyright © 2007, 2010 by Richard Salva
First edition published 2007. Second edition 2010
All rights reserved. Published 2010

Printed in the United States of America
ISBN: 978-1-56589-262-0
Epub ISBN: 978-1-56589-503-4

Cover art: Barbara Bingham
Cover design by Renée Glenn Designs, Nevada City, CA
Interior layout and design: Crystal Clarity Publishers
Photo credits: All Normandy photos by Richard and Laura Salva
Maps and diagrams by Richard Salva

Library of Congress Cataloging-in-Publication Data

Salva, Richard.
  Walking with William of Normandy : A Paramhansa Yogananda Pilgrimage Guide /
Richard Salva. -- 2nd ed.
    p. cm.
  ISBN 978-1-56589-262-0 (tradepaper)
  1. Normandy (France)--Guidebooks. 2. Normandy (France)--Description and travel. 3.
William I, King of England, 1027 or 8-1087--Homes and haunts--France--Normandy. 4.
Hindu pilgrims and pilgrimages. I. Title.

  DC611.N848S35 2010
  914.4'20484--dc22   2010041857

www.crystalclarity.com
clarity@crystalclarity.com
800-424-1055 or 530-478-7600

To William

PARAMHANSA YOGANANDA

[Paramhansa Yogananda] was lovable.... Yet he was also the very
personification of power!

—*Conversations with Yogananda* by Swami Kriyananda, p. 189.

Contents

Illustrations

Photographs

Maps and Diagrams

About the Maps

This book was originally published as an eBook. Using that format, it would be possible to zoom in on the maps for greater clarity.

To help you get the most out of these maps, I have created a webpage with downloads for each of them. Now you can download and zoom in on each map, just like those who have purchased the eBook version.

The Normandy Maps download webpage is:

www.crystarpress.com/bonus_stuff/w80W75w66maps.html

Please note: these maps are not intended as comprehensive place, city, or site descriptions. They are offered to enhance your awareness of where these sites are located in a given area. (For instance, very few of the street names are listed.) It is recommended, therefore, that you obtain tourist or other fully descriptive maps of any locations you are visiting, especially the cities of Caen, Bayeux, Lisieux, and Rouen.

A number of the maps I have made include site locations that are seldom or never listed on tourist maps, or are otherwise hard to find. They can be a helpful tool when used in conjunction with your other maps.

ACKNOWLEDGEMENTS

To everyone who helped with the development of this book, I express my deep and sincere thanks.

I would like to mention my appreciation toward:

The staff of the tourist offices for the cities of Caen, Touques, and Rouen in Normandy, France.

Jack Downey, for computer help.

My wife, Laura, who shared so much inspiration while walking with me in William's footsteps.

For other assistance: Swami Kriyananda, Asha and David Praver, Panduranga Heater, Rambhakta Beinhorn, Haridas Blake, and Frank Monahan.

I would especially like to thank Swami Kriyananda and Crystal Clarity Publishers for allowing the use of quotes from several works: *The New Path* and *Conversations with Yogananda*, by Swami Kriyananda, and *The Flawless Mirror* by Kamala Silva. Without their generous help, this book would not have been possible.

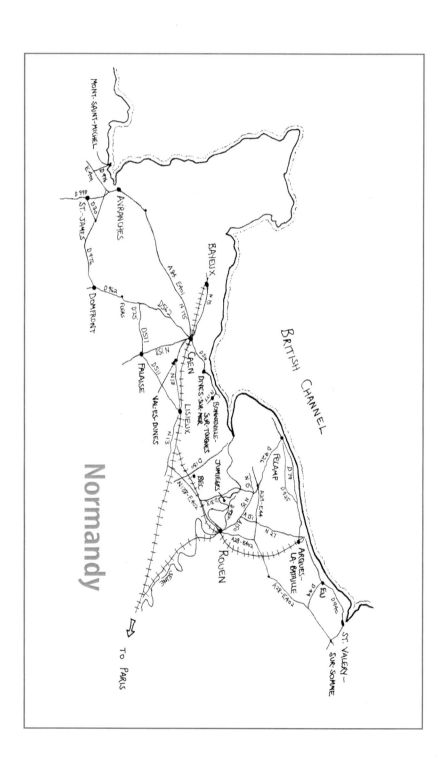

INTRODUCTION

Every year, followers of Paramhansa Yogananda—author of the spiritual classic, *Autobiography of a Yogi*—travel to India to meditate where that great master of yoga and other gurus of his lineage lived.

Yet there are similar pilgrimage spots in France that are seldom visited by yogis. These sites—blessed by Yogananda and Yogananda's guru, Sri Yukteswar—are located in Normandy. In fact, just a two-hour's train ride from Paris, one can find wonderful pilgrimage sites brimming with spiritual blessings.

I know. Years ago, my wife Laura and I included a week in Normandy as part of a trip to France. That week was the highlight of our trip. So much so that, two years later, we paid another visit.

The first time we went, we didn't know what to expect. Yogananda said that in a past life he had been the great Norman duke and British king, William the Conqueror, who lived in the eleventh century. Yogananda also said that his guru, Sri Yukteswar, had been Lanfranc—William's priest, counselor, and colleague.

(In addition, Swami Kriyananda, Yogananda's direct disciple, is convinced he was William's son, Henry I, in a past life. Historical evidence lends proof to this idea—see Catherine

Kairavi's excellent book, *Two Souls: Four Lives—The Lives and Former Lives of Paramhansa Yogananda and his disciple, Swami Kriyananda*.)

Laura and I wondered what our experience in Normandy would be like. Although we both felt a deep connection with Yogananda and his spiritual path, there was no guarantee we had lived in Normandy with William. Would these places mean that much to us? We pondered this question, never reflecting that most Yogananda followers who visit India probably hadn't lived with him there either. Nonetheless, they go there to feel the uplifting vibrations.

Similarly, it made sense that Yogananda's blessings would linger in places he had lived in any of his lifetimes, and that Yogananda devotees would feel those vibrations.

Kamala Silva was a direct disciple of Yogananda. In her book, *The Flawless Mirror*, Kamala wrote that Yogananda had told her, "of the divine magnetic qualities of saintly lives, and of holy places that can strongly influence those who are responsive." (*The Flawless Mirror*, p. 69)

Later, in that same book, Kamala described the powerful energy field that surrounded Yogananda. "I felt as if the sun's radiance was lighting the whole area. . . . How can one describe this spiritual force?" (Ibid, pp. 79-80)

In his autobiography, *The New Path*, Swami Kriyananda (another highly advanced, direct disciple) tells the story of Yogananda wading into the water at the recently purchased Lake Shrine in Pacific Palisades, California, and saying, "I am sending the divine light all through this lake." Later on, he informed the group of monk disciples that were with him, "This is holy water now. Whoever comes here in future will receive a divine blessing." (*The New Path*, p. 324)

Receptive souls who have visited places where Yogananda had lived or frequented (his family home in Calcutta, India; and Mt. Washington, Lake Shrine, Encinitas Ashram, Hollywood Church, etc., in California) have felt his powerful spiritual energy.

And yet, as I said, Laura and I were unsure what we would feel in Normandy. Probably, as some had suggested, a trip there would be more of a history lesson than anything else. What was our surprise, then, to feel a flood of spiritual blessings at these Normandy sites, to experience the same "spiritual force" Kamala described.

In our experience, these places may be compared in spiritual power with the most inspiring sites we have visited: Assisi, Lourdes, and Yogananda's shrines in California. The blessings were so transforming that we could have imagined ourselves in the Holy Land or one of the most sacred sites of India. And we became convinced that others who are open, and especially students of Yogananda's path of Self-realization, would also feel these Norman blessings.

As I wrote in my travel diary:

> Our pilgrimage to Normandy was an extraordinary experience, filled with deep inspiration. We walked where William had walked. We meditated in a church where Sri Yukteswar had served as the abbot. And we gazed at castle

walls built under the direction of Swami Kriyananda as Henry I.

We felt powerful, uplifting vibrations where virtually no one had prayed or meditated before. Places where, for centuries, the residents had no idea of their sanctity. Yet the spiritual vibrations in those places were very real.

Laura and I will never forget our Normandy pilgrimage. It was the sort of trip that changes lives.

If you feel a spiritual connection with Paramhansa Yogananda, I heartily recommend a visit to Normandy. If your experience is anything like ours, you will be more than glad you went.

Having been interested in William the Conqueror since I learned what Yogananda had said about him, I began to study historical texts. I also went to Great Britain in 1993 to see where the Battle of Hastings had taken place, and other William sites. Later, with my friend Tom Cerussi, I taught a class that presented evidence supporting Yogananda's words about his past life as William and exploring their significance.

One of the great things about Normandy is that many of the William sites are in small towns or the countryside. To a large degree the world has passed them by, leaving them relatively untouched, vibrationally.

I have been to other spiritual sites where so many worldly historical events had taken place in the same location, layered on top so to speak, that the spiritual energy present there took some inner digging to access. But in Normandy, with the exception of the relatively recent events of D-Day and World War II, the feeling was comparatively pristine. One could sense Yogananda as William, and Yukteswar as Lanfranc, without the intervening drama of the centuries.

Normandy as a European power dissolved soon after William and Lanfranc were there—almost as if the duchy had been created for their mission. In time, it was absorbed by France and became a backwater. Life, as I say, passed it by, and today many travel to Normandy for restful vacations. Cows grazing in lush pastures; pleasant woods; scenic drives; peaceful sea towns; the breeze blowing off the channel—these comprise an essential part of the Normandy experience. To go there, especially in the summer, is a treat.

This guidebook furnishes information that will help you plan and make a Normandy pilgrimage. Fortunately, Laura and I visited nearly every major William and Lanfranc site in the area—as well as a few other, more widely recognized pilgrimage spots—and all of those sites are described in this guide.

To give you some idea of what to expect, I have included maps, travel suggestions, basic tourist information, a little bit of history, photographs—and descriptions of our experiences, excerpted from my travel diary. For hotel accommodations and other information, check the regular guidebooks like Fodor's or Let's Go (or search online). In addition, I highly recommend the Michelin guide to Normandy. Also, since my maps are limited in detail, you might wish to purchase a Michelin road map of the heart of Normandy (#55 at the time

I purchased mine), and pick up supplementary city maps when you visit Caen, Rouen, and Lisieux.

The itinerary Laura and I followed worked very well. I recommend doing something similar, depending on your schedule.

Laura and I took the train from Paris to Caen, leaving from the Gare (station) St-Lazare, located north of the Champs-Elysees. (The Gares can be reached easily by taking the Metro, or Paris underground.) If you catch one of the faster trains, it should take little more than two hours to arrive in Caen—the city of William the Conqueror, and one of the best stops on the pilgrimage.

In Caen, we rented a car for a week, having made arrangements before leaving the States. (Cars are best for seeing Normandy. If you go solely by train, you miss half the sites.) If you decide to do this, bring an international driving license—French patrolmen expect you to have one—and study beforehand the street signs and driving customs of the French. Except for Bayeux, we drove to all the other pilgrimage sites: Dives, Mont-Saint-Michel, Falaise, Lisieux, Bec, Jumieges, and Rouen. From Rouen, we took the train back to Paris.

Using only the railway system, it is possible to see Caen, Bayeux, Lisieux, and Rouen. Trains from Caen to Rouen (which also stop in Lisieux) run daily and take about two hours. There are also departures from Caen to Paris that stop in Lisieux. The trains to Bayeux run on the Cherbourg line (Paris – Caen – Cherbourg).

RUE DE LA CONDEMME

ST. STEPHEN'S CHURCH

RUE AUX NAMS

CASTLE

MONASTERY FOR MEN

RUE ECUYERE

RUE SAINT PIERRE

RUE DES CHANOINES

RUE HAUTE

WOMEN'S MONASTERY

TRINITY CHURCH

RUE SAINT JEAN

CAEN

ORNE RIVER

TO DIVES

SAINT-MICHEL-DE-VAUCELLES CHURCH

RUE DE L'EGLISE ô.V.

RAILWAY STATION

RUE D'AUGE

TO FALAISE

SAINTE-PAIX CHURCH
RUE DU MARAIS

N

Chapter 1

CAEN

Laura and I loved Caen (pronounced "kawn"), a charming city in west-central Normandy. It hosts a wealth of Gothic church steeples, cobblestone streets, quaint shops—and Yogananda's blessings.

Our arrival in William the Conqueror's city was hectic. Seated on the train, Laura and I listened intently as the railway announcer spoke over the sound system, but we couldn't decipher his meaning. Luckily, a fellow passenger told us, with emphatic gestures, "Yes! This is Caen! You had better disembark now, before it is too late!"

We barely made it off the railway car before the train began to pull out of the station. I jumped onto the platform with a heavy suitcase clutched in my hand.

I was panting and testing my back for tweaks when Laura said, "It feels good here." I was surprised; then I stood still for a moment. She was right. It felt very good there. It felt like Yogananda.

Standing next to the tracks of a railway station located on the other side of the river and on the outskirts of a city that boasted its connection with William the Conqueror, Laura and I clearly felt the presence of Paramhansa Yogananda. It was the same powerful, uplifting energy we had felt at Yogananda's shrines and communities in California.

We immediately felt at home.

That feeling grew during our stay in Caen. It stole over us at unexpected moments, like St. Francis's presence in the streets of Assisi. At any moment, no matter what we were doing, suddenly we felt it—as if Yogananda were standing right there, blessing us. The vibration poured through like a divine tide, carrying away worldly concerns and replacing them with a deep experience of God.

The Caen railway station is on the southern edge of town. To arrive downtown, go north across the Orne River. If you wish to take a taxi, there is a terminal on the sidewalk just outside the station—look for the sign. There's often a queue of people waiting. Unfortunately, taxis don't come as frequently in Caen as they do in big cities, so you may have to wait a while. Other options are to rent a car from one of the agencies across the street from the station, or brave the bus system. Finally, if you've packed lightly and are in good physical condition, you can leg it—it's only a mile or two to downtown and all the sites and hotels.

Once you get settled, all the sites are in easy walking distance for most people. Try to pick a hotel that is centrally located. To make sure you have no problems finding accommodations,

I recommend arranging them before you leave. Then, confirm your reservations by phone soon before you arrive. You may also wish to avoid the crowds that visit Caen around June 6: the anniversary of D-Day.

If you can stay more than one day in Caen, I suggest that you do so. This was William's home for much of the time when he was in Normandy, and there is much to see and experience. Plus, you may wish to visit some sites more than once.

The Caen Tourist Office is located in Place Saint Pierre. For other information, visit:

www.francethisway.com/places/caen.php

WILLIAM'S CASTLE

Around the year 1050, William yearned for something more than what he had in Rouen, the traditional ducal city of Normandy. He wanted to create his own city, with his vibration and energy.

To the northwest, a small town at the confluence of the Orne and Odon rivers beckoned to him. William set down his roots there. He built a castle on a hill overlooking the town and made it his family abode. There, he and his wife and children would mainly reside when in Normandy.

William's castle, or chateau, stands in the center of Caen. Streets branch away from it, like arteries from the heart.

The Chateau de Caen (or Chateau Ducal; open daily, free admission) is beautiful and dramatic. (Guided tours in English are available for a fee, June 30 through September 7, Monday through Saturday, at 2:30 PM.) The castle rises on a hill above the center of town. Laura and I were enthralled.

We approached the chateau from the south. Its ramparts soared high above us as we walked the paths and lawns that grace its entrance. (The ramparts are not substantially different from those of William's time.) We shaded our eyes and gazed at the great white "Caen stone" walls that rose from the top of a natural mound of earth.

To enter the castle, follow the path that leads under a short wooden bridge and around and up in a great loop until you are facing the south gate. Cross the bridge and enter a bygone era.

(In William's day, the castle entrance was on the northern flank. One hundred thirty years later, it was moved to its current location.)

Inside, more green lawns will greet you, and a signboard map that shows the original castle layout. If you study the map, you will see several points of interest.

(First, ignore "Queen Matilda's Tower," off to your right. Despite being named after William's wife, it was built centuries later.)

Located just ahead of you on the main path is the church

of St-Georges. The current structure was erected three hundred years after William first began building here. But an earlier chapel stood at this site, circa 900s. It was still standing when William lived here, and the Norman duke almost certainly visited it, at least occasionally.

In fact, the parish of St-Georges took up a great deal of the total area of the original castle—which says a lot about William's attitude toward churches and spirituality.

(William and his family also had their own separate chapel, located next to where his original castle had stood.)

Forward and to the left of St-Georges is the Exchequer Hall, built by William's son, Henry I, and still intact. (The exchequer served as a sort of right-hand man and ducal accountant.)

Finally, and most importantly, to the right of Henry's exchequer are the ruins of William's original castle (the Old Palace, or "Vieux Palais"). These consist of a fenced-in square of blocks and chips of stone—beyond which lie the remains of a quadrangular keep (or "Donjon") built by Henry I to strengthen his father's castle.

THE RUINS OF WILLIAM'S PALACE

Following D-Day, there was a lot of fierce fighting in Caen. Eighty percent of the town was devastated. Consequently, some of what remains is in ruins.

If you wish to go directly there, William's chateau is located at the very back (left of center) of the property from where you enter the gate.

From my travel diary:

> At the beginning of our first visit, Laura and I made a beeline for the ruins of William's palace. We were walking along the sidewalk when I suddenly halted. A new dose of Yogananda's energy had touched my heart–the blessing that I have come to recognize as his. It was thrilling.
>
> We rested in a shaded area and discussed the beautiful inspiration we were feeling. Laura characterized it as a blend of what we'd experienced at Yogananda's shrines in Southern California, along with the Ananda Community in Northern California (founded by Yogananda's disciple, Swami Kriyananda, and dedicated to Yogananda and his spiritual path). The great yoga master was powerfully present.
>
> Laura and I meditated among the loose stones, the foundation blocks–all that remained of William's chateau. The walls might have fallen, but the vibrations seemed strong as ever.

INTERIOR VIEW OF WILLIAM'S PALACE RUINS

If possible, it is best to meditate on the actual ruins of William's original castle, where the blessings are strongest. To do so, you have to climb over a low wall (about two or three feet high). Wait for a moment when no one is around.

That said, remember that the current castle ramparts stand pretty much where they had in William's day. So he was familiar with every inch of these grounds. Yogananda said about his "castle on a hill" home in Los Angeles–Mt. Washington–that he had meditated on and spiritually blessed every part of those grounds. (*The New Path*, pp. 324-25) If you are interrupted while meditating in or near William's old palace, I recommend finding another quiet corner to continue. ("Where there's a 'Will,' there's a way!")

For more information about William's Chateau, see:
www.chateau.caen.fr/ANGLAIS/Historique/index.htm

St. Stephen's Church and the Men's Monastery

While standing on the grounds of William's castle, next to the exterior wall, one can look out over the wall and view the town below. Caen has been dubbed the "city of spires," and there are many gothic steeples that rise above the other buildings. (This is deeply appropriate, for Caen was William's city and William was a church builder.)

If you gaze west from those walls, you will see a building with twin spires. Those spires form part of the roofline of the church of St. Stephen's (Saint-Etienne), behind which lies the Monastery for Men (L'Abbaye aux Hommes). These combined make the second great William the Conqueror site in Caen.

St. Stephen's

When William married his distant cousin, Matilda, the church disapproved. This estrangement with the Vatican weighed on William's mind, and he sent his friend and counselor Lanfranc (Sri Yukteswar) to Rome to argue his case. As you can imagine, the wise and diplomatic Lanfranc was successful (it probably helped that he was born in Italy), and the pontiff lifted the sanction. Part of the agreement was that William and Matilda would build two monasteries: one on behalf of William for men, and one on Matilda's behalf for women (both begun around 1060). The monastery church for men was named St. Stephen's, and William so loved it that he asked to be buried there.

It doesn't take long to reach St. Stephen's from the castle—about fifteen or twenty minutes if you walk fast. Laura and I had to hurry the first time because it was about to close. Its hours are from 8:15 AM to noon and 2 to 7:30 PM, daily.

But if you aren't in a rush, the streets and shops of Caen are charming. There are open plazas with statues and historic markers: reminders of William or of World War II. And across the street from the castle is the Caen tourist office where they have local maps and booklets on the Conqueror.

There are also quite a few restaurants. Many, of course, serve Norman cuisine (which is heavy into seafood), but we also found a Chinese restaurant, and even a Mexican one. Street vendors sell sandwiches on French baguettes. (When I bit into one, I was pleasantly surprised. I never expected a vendor-bought cheese sandwich could be so flavorful!)

To arrive at St. Stephen's from William's Castle, exit the Chateau gate (there's only one entry and exit). Across the street (Rue Saint Pierre) is an old Gothic church. Turn right on Rue Saint Pierre, and keep going for about five blocks. Then, take a gradual right onto Rue Ecuyere. Stay on that road, and when the street name changes to Rue Guillaume le Conquérant, you will see the church of St. Stephen's on your left. Search along its walls for the dark-painted plywood door.

The St. Stephen complex includes both a church, and a monastery next to the church. Parts of the church hail from William's time, but the current monastery buildings were erected much later (eighteenth century), and are now used for local government offices. (Tours of the monastery are available; I found the experience interesting, but not deeply inspiring. Inside the monastery is a statue of William, whose grimacing face resembles the actor Charlton Heston.)

During our first visit, Laura and I focused on the church.

We headed straight for the altar. A little ways behind it—set in the floor of the choir and raised slightly above the walkway—was the large, inscribed, rectangular marble block that lies atop William's tomb. We touched the stone for William's blessing, then sat to meditate on the step that juts out in front of his tomb.

HENRY'S
DONJON

CAFE

ST. GEORGE'S
CHURCH

ENTRY

REMAINS OF
WILLIAM'S
PALACE

EXCHEQUER BLDG.

CAEN
CASTLE

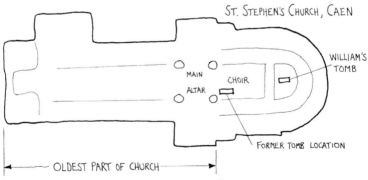

ST. STEPHEN'S CHURCH, CAEN

MAIN
ALTAR

CHOIR

WILLIAM'S
TOMB

FORMER TOMB LOCATION

OLDEST PART OF CHURCH

**SITE OF WILLIAM'S TOMB, AND HIS TOMBSTONE,
ST. STEPHEN'S**

At first I felt spiritually out-of-synch. I had been focusing, as I thought proper, on William who had loved this church; but I felt inwardly blocked. A piece of the puzzle was missing.

Suddenly, enlightenment came. Lanfranc. St. Stephen's church and monastery had been under his direction. He had served as its abbot. William was so appreciative of Lanfranc and everything the great monk had done to help his work that he insisted Lanfranc accept the keys to St. Stephen's. In a past life, Sri Yukteswar had served God in this building. As soon as I made that mental connection and concentrated on Lanfranc, a wave of grace descended. In my heart, I thanked Sri Yukteswar for his blessings.

Basking in an inner glow, I thought gratefully: "What a town!" Here in Caen, we had found powerful sacred sites related to the past lives of two avatars—Yogananda and Sri Yukteswar—within a short walking distance of each other. What other city in the Western Hemisphere could make such a claim? Caen, I reflected, is truly a Mecca for devotees.

Notes: While speaking with the locals, I learned that William's father, Duke Robert the Magnificent, sent back from the Holy Land a small part of St. Stephen's finger as a sacred relic to be enshrined in St. Stephen's church. Later, William himself bought, for the same purpose, St. Stephen's arm and one of the stones that had killed him. (St. Stephen was the first Christian martyr—killed for his faith. He was stoned to death in Jerusalem soon after Christ's crucifixion and resurrection.)

William's crypt used to lie in a different location—still in the choir, but almost immediately behind the central altar of the church. His bodily remains were buried there for nearly five hundred years. But the tower above (made of wood and named the Lantern Tower) collapsed in the sixteenth century, damaging the choir area and William's Tomb. At that time, they moved his sarcophagus to its current spot.

Oddly enough, Laura and I felt more of William's blessings near the current tomb than the original site, even though it is unclear whether any of William's remains still lie beneath his tombstone. His remains were dispersed during the religious wars of the 1560s, and later. (Conflicting reports say either that

William's thighbone still lies in his crypt, or that it was the last body part taken during the French Revolution.)

St. Stephen's is a functioning church, and there may be a Catholic Mass in progress when you enter. But we found that those services often take place in a side chapel away from William's tomb, leaving us relatively free to make our private devotions.

However, if you are visiting the tomb while Mass is being celebrated in the main part of the church, you will be visible behind the altar and a distraction for those attending service. If you find yourself in this situation, I suggest that you take a seat in a choir pew and quietly meditate until the Mass has ended. Earplugs and the practice of *pratyahara* (sense withdrawal) are recommended.

You may wish to take a tour of St. Stephen's Church. These tours depart from the main hall of the abbey, next to the church. If you go into the main entryway you will see the signs advertising tours. Check before you go that the tour you are taking will encompass the church (daily at 9:30 AM and 2:30 and 4 PM); some focus solely on the history of the abbey (daily at 11 AM).

Other William Sites in Caen

Another site in Caen that may be of interest is the church of Our Lady of the Trinity (Notre-Dame de la Trinité) and the Monastery for Women (L'Abbaye aux Dames). This site is located on the opposite side of the castle from St. Stephen's—to the east rather than west. William's wife, Matilda, was buried there in 1083 (in the church choir); one of William's daughters (Cecilia) entered the convent at a young age and later served as its abbess; and one may assume that William frequently visited the site during the building phase and after. In fact, the Duke and his companions attended the church's dedication on June 18, 1066, shortly before setting sail for England. The Abbey buildings currently house regional council offices. (The church is open Monday through Saturday, 8 AM to 6 PM, and Sunday, 9:30 AM to 12:30 PM. The abbey is open daily from 2 to 5:30 PM.)

I visited Our Lady of the Trinity during my second trip to Normandy, but I didn't receive much inspiration there. To me it felt empty, especially near Matilda's tomb. I found some inspiration in the gardens adjoining the monastery buildings (those gardens used to belong to the abbey); but there wasn't a strong feeling of William's presence. It was more of a general feeling of religious upliftment—what one might expect to feel in *any* building that used to house a convent. But your experience may be different.

I recommend that, when in Caen, you visit William's chateau and St. Stephen's church first. Then, if you have time, try the Trinity Convent.

(If you feel William's presence there, I would like to hear about it. Write me at: info@CrystarPress.com.)

To get to the Women's Monastery from William's Castle is easy. When you exit the castle, turn left onto the street in front of you and continue for a few blocks. At one point, the street branches into two avenues: Rue des Chanoines (on the left) and Rue Haute (on the right). Either one of those two streets will take you to the monastery. It's about a fifteen-minute walk, much of it uphill.

Just a block away from the Caen train station, on the corner of Rue d'Auge and Rue du Marais, stands a church that William ordered built in 1047. The church, named Sainte-Paix (or Holy Peace), was intended to commemorate a treaty called the Truce of God. The church building has suffered from many upheavals through the centuries. Today, of the original structure, only the choir section still stands.

If you take a taxi from the Caen railway station, you might ask the driver to stop by "l'Eglise de Sainte-Paix" on your way downtown. Or you might prefer to visit the church before catching a taxi. It only takes a few minutes to walk there.

Likewise, there is another church not far from the Caen train station called Saint-Michel-de-Vaucelles. It also lies south of the river, on the Rue de l'Eglise de Vaucelles. History shows that William visited this church and probably worshipped in it. Like Sainte-Paix, you might take a taxi from the train station and visit Saint-Michel on your way downtown. Alternately, you can take a cab from the city to the church after you are settled in. If you are athletic and feel like stretching your legs after your train-ride into Caen, you might visit both Sainte-Paix and Michel-de-Vaucelles on foot (they look to be about ten minutes apart), and then hike into the city.

I will mention in passing another location in Caen that may draw die-hard William fans. At 2 Rue aux Namps (located about midway between William's castle and St. Stephen's Church) is a building that, according to local tradition, stands on the site where William the Conqueror's half-brother, Bishop Odo, had a residence. As I just learned of this site recently, I cannot say what you might experience there.

During my stay in this special city, I found that it didn't matter whether I was on the grounds of an old church or castle; I found William in every street of Caen. On the last morning of my first visit—a Sunday—the shops were closed and I walked blissfully through the empty streets singing Yogananda's chant "Door of My Heart" in French. I felt as inspired as if I were attending a Yogananda-based worship service.

My most uplifting moments in Caen were meditating in the ruins of William's castle and pressing my forehead to his grave in St. Stephen's.

For more about Caen's history, see: www.channel4.com/history/microsites/H/history/e-h/harold06.html

(For a William site about thirty minutes outside of Caen, Val-és-Dunes, see Chapter 11: Off the Beaten Track—Other William Sites in Normandy.)

Chapter 2

Bayeux

Two years after our first visit to Normandy, Laura and I returned. We enjoyed many of the sites we had visited before, plus I added a few more, including Bayeux.

Bayeux is a small town, smaller even than Caen. It is especially noteworthy as the home of the Bayeux Tapestry, but it has other William connections as well.

Bayeux can be reached by train out of the Caen station. It is the next stop on the Paris-Caen line. It takes less than twenty minutes to get there. When I went, it cost about eight dollars each way.

When you arrive, you have a choice of hiking twenty minutes or so into town from the train depot–which is located on the outskirts–or you can take one of the taxis that pull up regularly outside of the station.

The Cathedral

The city's principal landmark, whose spires loom above you as you approach downtown, is the Cathedral Notre-

Dame de Bayeux. This old stone church witnessed many historical moments. It was completed in 1077 and William attended its official consecration. In addition, William's half-brother Odo served as bishop here. (The crypt and sections of the west towers remain from that time.)

It is also worth mentioning that Harold of England swore allegiance to William on sacred relics in an earlier church at this location. Harold was William's nemesis during the Battle of Hastings.

(Decades before, renegade Norman nobles also swore on those same relics to kill young William. Clearly if anyone intends to keep an oath, they should steer clear of those relics!)

William's friendship with Bishop Odo of Bayeux ran hot and cold. Odo participated in William's conquest of England, but in time William would imprison his power-hungry brother—who was conniving to become Pope—for four years. In fact, it took the pleas of William's followers to convince the dying duke and king to free Odo. With these undercurrents, and given that Bayeux is only fifteen miles from Caen, William must have come here often.

I visited Bayeux in the month of June, and it was a pleasure to escape the heat by stepping into the cathedral's cool entrance. While sitting in the church I could feel William's presence as a deep peace. The Bayeux Cathedral is architecturally beautiful and a pleasant place to rest and meditate. I recommend that you take your time and enjoy it.

The Bayeux Cathedral hours are: January 1 through March 31, from 8:30 AM to 5 PM; April 1 through June 30, from 8:30 AM to 6 PM; July 1 through September 30, from 8:30 AM to 7 PM; and October 1 through December 31, from 8:30 AM to 6 PM.

The Tapestry

From the cathedral, it is only a short walk to the Bayeux Tapestry.

As you exit the church, turn left and walk until you reach Rue de Nesmond. Turn left on that street, and follow it downhill. After you pass over a stream, you will see the Tapestry Museum (Centre Culturel Guillaume le Conquérant) on your left.

These directions are very simple, but if for any reason you find that you have lost your way, watch for directing signs saying "La Tapisserie" or "La Tapisserie de la Reine Mathilde." (Bayeux wisely ensures that its major tourist attraction won't be missed!)

(The Tapestry Museum's hours are: March 15 through April 30, from 9 AM to 6:30 PM; May 1 through August 31, from 9 AM to 7 PM; September 1 through November 2, from 9 AM to 6:30 PM; November 3 through March 14, from 9:30 AM to 12:30 PM and from 2 PM to 6 PM. The Museum is closed the second week in January, from Monday through Friday.)

As you venture into the heart of Bayeux, you may imagine that you have passed through a time portal. Bayeux is probably one of the most well-preserved medieval towns in Europe. It escaped the devastation that the aftermath of D-Day inflicted on Caen and other Norman cities. The Germans and Allies pretty much drove straight past Bayeux, choosing to fight elsewhere. Anyone who loves stone bridges and buildings, cobblestone streets, old wooden shutters, and windowsills festooned with bright and colorful sprays of flowers will enjoy Bayeux.

After you enter the Tapestry Museum and pay the entrance fee (about eight dollars when I went), you will be taken on a historical tour of Normandy in the Middle Ages. Throughout the museum are displays and dioramas, and even a short film intended to help you understand and appreciate the Tapestry and the times in which it was made.

(Strictly speaking, it isn't really a tapestry, but a work of embroidery. Somebody christened it with this misnomer and it stuck.)

The Tapestry itself is on the ground floor, but before seeing it, you will be directed up the stairway to the floors above. On the second floor (called first floor in France), you will learn about the Vikings (Norman ancestors), along with a detailed examination and study of the Tapestry (copied in sections). You will also discover what England was like in William's day. The third floor (called second floor) tells the story of William's wife, Queen Matilda, and William's brother, Odo.

All of the displays are educational, and it can be fun to guess whether this work was commissioned by Odo, or William's wife Matilda. But for me, none of the opening acts compared with the tapestry itself.

It seems strange to say so, but I actually felt awe when I saw it. I suppose it's possible that I had seen the Tapestry before, and that a past-life familiarity added to its magic. But it really is an amazing work of art. The cartoonish figures are oddly endearing. And, maybe it's just me, but I seem to see Yogananda's aquiline nose in the multiple and easy-to-spot depictions of William.

William himself must have seen this embroidery many times. That was apparently one of the main reasons for producing it—to present William with a record or memento of that major achievement of his life.

There are good reasons to suppose that Odo commissioned the work. Notice how often the bishop is shown at William's side, as if to say, "Don't forget that I was there when you needed me. I stood by you even in the most difficult times!"

Odo was strikingly different from a modern bishop. For one thing, in addition to being a churchman, he was a mace-wielding warrior.

The Bayeux Tapestry also served as propaganda for the Norman cause. It was probably created in England by British craftsmen and women. Recent studies suggest that they may have hidden some anti-Norman propaganda in the work.

For more on the tapestry, see: www.hastings1066.com/

By the way, the Tapestry Museum is an excellent place to go shopping. Its gift shop sells lots of items displaying images from the tapestry (magnets, bookmarks, mugs, t-shirts, etc.). (This Christmas, give the gift of William!)

Near Bayeux: for anyone who would like to experience an overnight stay in a building originally built by William's half-brother Odo (between 1074 and 1077), Chateau de Neuilly is situated within an hour's drive of Bayeux.

To explore this unusual Norman lodging opportunity, and for descriptions, directions, and prices, see: www.chateauneuilly.com/index.html

Chapter 3

Dives-sur-Mer

The Dives is a river on the Normandy coast that flows into the English Channel. Dives-sur-Mer is a small town that rests on the point where those waters merge, about twenty-five kilometers from Caen.

Dives has a powerful association with William the Conqueror. For it was here that William gathered his forces for his invasion of Britain, and it was from here that he first set sail to cross the Channel. (He also fought and won an important battle at this site, years before his conquest of England.)

To get to Dives, drive northeast from Caen on Highway D 513 (watch the road signs, the highway curves around a little). After about forty-five minutes, you will see a sign on your right-hand side saying "Dives-sur-Mer." Go straight ahead into the residential and business area, and park as soon as you can find a spot somewhere along the street. Then you'll need to hike back, walking along the right-hand side of the road as you go west. You will see a little shop, something like a 7-Eleven, on your right, and just before you get to that shop, a little field with a dirt path. Turn right onto the dirt path, walking north toward the sea.

THE AVENUE BESIDE THE DIVES RIVER

(If you're still on the road and have reached the Dives sign, or the bridge over the Dives River, turn back; you've gone too far.)

The narrow path will take you to a wider avenue that follows the banks of the river. Keep walking north on the path, with the river on your left. This is where the magic takes place—or at least it did for Laura and me when we were there.

From my travel diary:

> As we walked along the river, it wasn't long before that same feeling we had sensed in Caen descended on us. Yogananda was near.

Laura and I agreed to experience this site in silence and to share our impressions later. It was curious because, even though we were generally in the right area, neither of us knew exactly where the ancient encampment had been. Yet the feeling of divine energy grew incredibly strong at one section of the embankment right by the river: as if we were passing through an invisible vibrational wall. The feeling sustained for a while, then grew more faint the farther we walked. When in the midst of it, I was sure I was standing on the same ground William's soldiers had inhabited—where they had loaded up the ships for their journey to England—the image depicted on the Bayeaux Tapestry. It seemed odd because, even though this was basically just an old military site, I felt as if I were standing in Jerusalem or Benares. The inspiration was that strong.

We sat by the river to meditate.

Laura put her experience into words, "I felt joy and peace, and a strong sense of divine reassurance."

It puzzled me why this ground should hold such a powerful divine energy, and I tried to think it through, to reconstruct what had happened.

Back in 1066, William called his military leaders and their knights to sail their newly built ships to this spot, along with anyone else he could induce to come: Flemish and French soldiers, and mercenaries. According to the records, at one point

William had all the men, ships, horses, supplies, and portable castle walls in place, but then the weather refused to cooperate. The wind was blowing in the wrong direction, and it continued that way for quite some time. Meanwhile the men sat here waiting. Days and weeks passed by while they waited.

In the end, they remained in Dives for a month and a half. William visited this site often during that period, but stayed mostly at a castle in Bonneville, about ten miles east as the seagulls fly. There, along with his barons, he fine-tuned his invasion plans. But he must have been keenly aware of the situation in the encampment.

Many of the Norman soldiers would have had mixed feelings. This was a dangerous expedition, a great risk. They might all drown in the channel, be killed in a foreign land, or come back with nothing. Many of them had homes nearby that beckoned. Dives is located in the very heart of Normandy. While they waited here, it would have been easy to brood on the foolhardiness of the venture, and the wisdom, the common sense, even, of returning to their wives and children, their hearths and homes.

And then there were the foreigners and mercenaries. Those men were held by even feebler ties. It would have been difficult to keep such a loose confederation focused on the goal. With the lack of activity, it would have been natural for the men to grumble and complain—and leave.

This long delay was one of the most delicate moments in the history of the Norman invasion of England. The whole venture hung by a thread. Over those weeks, William's army could easily have dispersed by ones, twos, and small groups. In the end, he might have been left with only a token force.

But William was more than just a great leader. He was a spiritual master. He was Yogananda in a past life, and he knew what to do.

Paramhansa Yogananda often spoke of how he would send his thoughts and energy to his disciples. Even when they were many miles away, those disciples were able to feel and experience his inner messages.

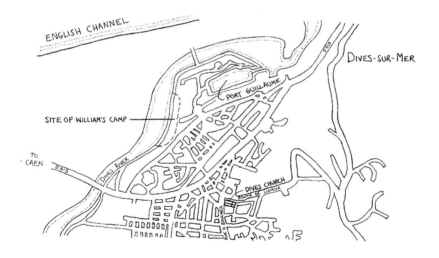

In letters that Yogananda sent to Kamala Silva, he wrote, "[I] spiritually bless you every day." (*The Flawless Mirror*, p. 89) and, "Many, many times I send you a thousand blessings through God." (Ibid, p. 95)

In Chapter Nine of *The Flawless Mirror*, Kamala describes some of the many spiritual experiences Yogananda sent her from a distance–light, sound, joy, peace, and currents of spiritual energy. (Ibid, p. 99) She also mentions how the great master had strongly conveyed to her a thought or idea through his will. (Ibid, p. 104)

Similarly, William the Conqueror sent a powerful thought-form to Dives. To ensure that everyone stayed put and remained in tune, and that the invasion would go forth as planned, he cast his brilliant aura over the encampment. Hour after hour, day after day, week after week, he projected his energy, consciousness, purpose, and will to that spot. And some nine hundred and thirty-five years later, Laura and I felt that energy in Dives. William's spiritual power had sustained through the centuries. It was more than tangible; it was overwhelming.

Dives is an amazing place. As I sat there with my eyes closed, I felt as if I were in some great and sacred temple. Then I opened my eyes and saw on my right a nondescript open field, and to my left a swampy riverbank. Maybe someone will build a temple there someday. The astral temple (the most important part) was constructed long ago.

If you keep going north, you will spot, ahead of you and to your left, a walking bridge that crosses the river. (I felt Yogananda's energy beginning about halfway along the path between the main road and the bridge. The vibrations ended just south of the bridge.) Where the bridge meets the shore,

THE AUTHOR, MEDITATING AT DIVES

there is a sign advertising a housing settlement on the east bank of the river. The settlement is named after William (Place Guillaume). Laura and I walked through the settlement and to the docks on the northern side (Port Guillaume), where there was a café. We ordered a meal and enjoyed the view. Laura and I were so inspired by the vibrations and scenery of Dives that we discussed moving there someday.

Also in Dives: There is another William site that Laura and I were unaware of and missed. According to tradition, William and his men attended mass at the Dives church (L'Eglise Notre Dame de Dives) before they set sail for England. (After departing from Dives, they traveled east along the Normandy coast before crossing the channel.) In fact, there is a plaque in that Dives church with a list of those who accompanied William in his conquest. (As you can imagine, that plaque is revered by genealogists.)

Much of the current church was built in the fourteenth and fifteenth centuries, but the walls of the chapel itself went up during the reign of William's father, Duke Robert. If you visit Dives, I highly recommend stopping to meditate at this church—centrally located at the corner of Route de Lisieux and Rue Helene Boucher.

The town of Dives advertises an arts and crafts section, also named after William (Le Village d'art Guillaume le Conquérant). We saw the sign as we drove in. (If you go there, you may choose to dine at eateries with historic names like Le Hastings or Restaurant Guillaume.)

I don't know whether the craft shops sell anything connected with the Norman Conquest; we didn't have time to stop. But, just as in Caen, the people of Dives seem quite proud of their association with the Conqueror. Not surprisingly, William is remembered with more affection in Normandy than in England.

You can find out more about the town of Dives-sur-Mer by accessing the website below (WARNING: with these "translated from the French" pages, you sometimes have to read between the lines): http://tinyurl.com/33jzo3

Chapter 4

BONNEVILLE-SUR-TOUQUES

Since you've come this far, I may as well mention another
William site a half-hour farther east along the coast. Bonneville
was where William stayed while all the activity was happening in
Dives, and the castle where he dwelled—or rather, what's left of it—
is still there, and named "Le Chateau des Ducs de Normandie."

Laura and I had quite an adventure finding the place. The
only problem was that it was closed to the public. The castle
stands on privately owned land, with a locked gate and a fence
that shuts off the view, and what sounds like a massive dog on
the other side. We managed to get the attention of someone
who worked there, but in spite of our pleas she was unwill-
ing to let us even glimpse the castle through the gate from
the road. The extent of our experience of this site was feeling
Yogananda's presence as we hiked up to it, standing for a few
moments of relative silence (growling, barking dog) in front of
the gate, and a brief glimpse of the chateau from the other side
of the road.

If you'd like to make an attempt to see the castle, I recommend several things. First, if you can speak French and have

a persuasive personality, you might call ahead to see if they will let you in. (You can get the phone number at the tourist center in Touques.) Second, perhaps a small group will have better success than just two people. Third, be sure to drive all the way to Bonneville and not hike up the hill from the town of Touques below. It's a pretty strenuous climb (as Laura and I discovered).

BONNEVILLE CASTLE FROM THE ROADSIDE

To get to Bonneville-sur-Touques from Dives, continue east on Highway D 513, then turn south in Deauville onto Highway N 177. Follow the signs into Touques, then ask for directions to Bonneville at the tourist center downtown.

To view pictures of the Bonneville castle ruins go to:
http://tinyurl.com/2nehth

Then click on each shot for an enlargement.

Chapter 5

Mont-Saint-Michel and Avranches

You have probably seen photographs of this beautiful monastery, dramatically ensconced on an island hill. Before heading south and east to the other principal William sites in Normandy, Laura and I took a day to drive west and visit Mont-Saint-Michel, and you may wish to do the same. There are good arguments for doing so. Not only is it an interesting medieval monastery, but William's son, Henry I, was in charge of it at one point. (He was actually besieged here by his brothers.) The mount is also pictured on the Bayeaux Tapestry, so William definitely came here. Beyond that, there is a Lanfranc connection: the great monk lived and taught either in the nearby town of Avranches or in the island monastery itself before he moved east to the Abbey of Bec, where he met William.

The monastery's origins are inspired. It was founded in the eighth century by Bishop Aubert of Avranches, who had repeated visions of St. Michael the Archangel urging him to build a church on the island hill. He finally gave in, and over the centuries this famous monastery, named after the angel/saint, came into being. Laura and I felt an angelic presence in the chapel. (The southern part of the nave dates from William's era.)

MONT-SAINT-MICHEL

SAINT MICHAEL STATUE, MONT-SAINT-MICHEL

The Abbey is open from May 2 through August 31, from 9 AM to 7 PM (last admission at 6 PM); and from September 1 through April 30, from 9:30 AM to 6 PM (last admission at 5 PM). It is closed on New Year's Day, May 1, and Christmas Day.

While driving to Mont-Saint-Michel, you will pass through Avranches. The city has an old ruined castle, built in the ninth century, that William used to visit. At that time it was inhabited by Hugh the Wolf, Viscount d'Avranches, one of William's companions in his Conquest of England. The castle, which is open to the public, is supposed to be centrally located downtown. It stands on a hill. I couldn't find it on a map, but I imagine that if you drove into town, it wouldn't take long to spot. One could always roll down the window and inquire, "Ou est le chateau, si'l vous plait?" ("Oo ay luh sha-toe, see voo play?") Or, "Where is the castle, please?"

Frankly, I wish Laura and I had had more time to explore Avranches. I have a feeling it would have been one of the highlights of our trip. As it was, when we passed through the city, we merely stopped by the roadside for a brief meditation.

To arrive at Mont-Saint-Michel from Caen, drive west on highway N 175. (I have also seen this highway listed as A 84-E 401. Either way, the destination signs should list Avranches and/or Mont-Saint-Michel.) This route will take you within a few miles of the monastery. After you pass through Avranches, follow the signs for the turnoff to the right that will take you to the Mount, or rather the parking lot below. Expect a strenuous climb from the island's base to the monastery peak.

If you go, be sure to leave Caen early in the day. It's a long drive, and when we went, only part of the route was a freeway—there were long stretches of two-lane highways and more modest roads. But the scenery is pleasant, and all the land between Caen and the Mount was subject to William's rule.

In fact, if you're visiting both Mont-Saint-Michel and Avranches, you may want to stay overnight at one of the two locations. Mont-Saint-Michel would probably be uplifting but expensive; Avranches is most likely cheaper.

Websites:
www.mont-saint-michel.monuments-nationaux.fr/en/
www.en.wikipedia.org/wiki/Mont_Saint_Michel
www.ot-avranches.com/en/pageLibre00010430.htm

Nearby: South of Avranches, and forming a triangle with Avranches and Mont-Saint-Michel, is a town with Conqueror connections. Saint-James hosts a famous WW II cemetery, but it has eleventh-century roots as well. William fortified the town during his years of trouble with nearby Brittany, and there is supposed to be a "William the Conqueror walk" along the remains of the old town wall. If you go, ask in the tourist office about the William walk.

To get to Saint-James from Mont-Saint-Michel, drive north on N 175 toward Avranches. Take the D 998 exit going south. Drive for about five miles and look for the signs.

Chapter 6

Falaise

If you stand in front of William's Castle in Caen and look southeast down Rue St.-Jean, that street (which changes into highway N 158) goes straight to the Conqueror's birthplace in Falaise. No doubt William used an early version of this road many times. The trip from Caen to Falaise takes about an hour.

When you exit the highway into Falaise, just follow the signs to the castle (Chateau Guillaume-Le-Conquérant), or you can use the imposing building itself as a compass. (The town is rather small.) Park in the square below the castle.

The castle hours are: February 10 through June 30, from 10 AM to 6 PM; July 1 through August 31, from 10 AM to 7 PM; September 1 through December 31, from 10 AM to 6 PM. Last tickets are sold one hour before closing. It is closed Christmas Day.

FALAISE CASTLE

From my travel diary:

We pulled into Falaise around noon. Because of road-work and detours, it took a while to find the town square at the base of the castle hill.

Laura and I hiked up the hill and were rewarded by the romantic sight of the old chateau's partially ruined outer walls.

In 1944, Allied tanks chased Nazi Panzers right through the heart of William's birthplace. Much of the town was devastated, and it soon became clear that the castle had not escaped damage. Only a shell of the original remained.

As we hiked through the main gate, Laura and I enjoyed the sight of the cylindrical tower that hove into view from behind a hill. Soon, we were walking up a metal ramp to the castle entrance, and it struck me how much work the people of Falaise had put into the place. One could imagine the skeleton of a building they were left with after World War II. But now we saw that half of the castle consisted of metal walls and walkways, or cement made to blend in with the old stonework.

After buying our tickets and receiving our headphones, Laura and I pushed on the large front door (reminiscent of the front doors to the Wizard of Oz's palace). It opened into a grand salon: the first of many stops on a guided audio-tour called "From Legend to History."

The first room, with its blank walls and mirrored floor panels, looked like something out of a science fiction tale. Ivory and ebony chessboards and multiple screens were laid

out. The screens were used for slide images that correspond-
ed with the audio-monologue as presented in the headsets
we were given at the door. There were similar scenes in the
rooms we visited next. Each story had to do with royalty who
had lived in, or had some historic experience related to, that
particular room. It turned out that this first room was located
in a tower built by Henry I, who, as in Caen, had reinforced
the castle his father (William the Conqueror) was born in.
(Similar, I thought, to what Swami Kriyananda has done in
this life, reinforcing the foundations and structure of his guru
Paramhansa Yogananda's spiritual work.)

The slide productions and monologues were excellent.
Laura and I enjoyed watching and listening as we made our
way through winding passageways, long courtrooms, and high
towers. We heard about Queen Eleanor of Aquitaine, King
Philippe-Auguste of France, and others. But they saved the
best for last.

The final salon presented the story of William the Conqueror,
with slides projected past waist-high models of water-borne
ships. We learned details of William's life that brought him
more fully to life and helped us appreciate what he went
through in his early years. (For me, especially, it was gratify-
ing to hear his story told sympathetically; nearly all the books
I had read in my studies of William were lukewarm toward
him, at best.)

After this rendition, the lights went up. As we turned
around, we saw that William's story was also presented on tab-
lets arrayed along the walls. Each tablet furnished the essence

of an important moment in William's life. As we circled the room clockwise, we got the full picture.

Beyond the educational value, there was deep inspiration in this room. Laura and I walked reverently from one display to the next. For this room, apparently, contained remnants of the building in which William was born in 1027.

Afterward, as we sat on a grassy knoll facing the palace, Laura told me how stirred she had been by the presentation, and how she had felt for the first time a deep connection with William's life. She was moved to tears as she heard of the many people who had tried to kill William when he was a boy.

I understood what she meant. Sitting on the grass, meditating, I felt a sweetness that reminded me of Swami Kriyananda's words in his Holy Land Oratorio, when he described Jesus' birth in Bethlehem and the descent of God to earth, like a light piercing through clouds of darkness.

God also came to Falaise; Yogananda's spirit was born there to fulfill a divine mission. And I realized once again the spiritual power that surrounds the historic life of the Conqueror—a power that sensitive souls can feel and appreciate—a power unsuspected by most historians, even those inspired by William.

Also in Falaise: Following his conquest of England, William ordered the building of a church in the town where he was born, and named it Saint-Gervais. This church, which was finished by Henry I, is located in the heart of Falaise. Definitely worth a visit.

PARAMHANSA YOGANANDA

Falaise web pages:
www.chateau-guillaume-leconquerant.fr/web/histoire_uk.php
www.world66.com/europe/france/normandybrittany/falaise
freespace.virgin.net/doug.thompson/normandy/falaise.htm

A disciple of [Paramhansa Yogananda] was reading [William the Conqueror's] life once, and came upon a passage where William was described as courting Matilda by knocking her down and dragging her about the room by the hair. Amused, the disciple read the section aloud to the Master. He replied in amazement, "How they distort history! What happened wasn't like that at all."

—*Conversations with Yogananda* by Swami Kriyananda, pp. 192-93.

Lisieux

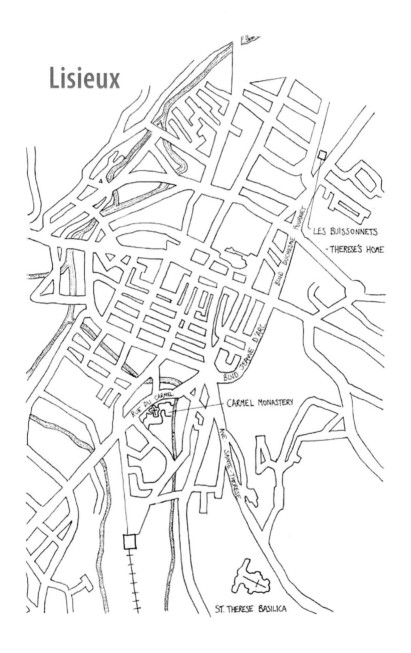

LES BUISSONNETS
- THERESE'S HOME

BLVD DUCHESNE

BLVD JEANNE D'ARC

RUE AU CARMEL

CARMEL MONASTERY

AVE SAINTE THERESE

ST. THERESE BASILICA

Chapter 7

Lisieux

What spiritual seeker on pilgrimage would pass up a town dedicated to a saint? Besides, Lisieux lies directly between two William sites: Falaise and Bec.

To arrive in Lisieux (pronounced "lee-zoo"), drive northeast from Falaise on highway D 511, then turn east onto highway N 13. It takes a good hour or more to get there.

Lisieux was made famous by Thérèse—a much-loved Catholic saint who lived from 1873 to 1897, and was well known for her sweet and simple devotion to Christ. For William-trackers, Lisieux has another interest, for it was the seat of one of the episcopal sees in the Conqueror's day, encompassing the two monasteries William and his wife had built in Caen. William was well acquainted with the bishop of Lisieux. Furthermore, the duke attended and, indeed, convened nearly every meeting of the church leaders, and several took place here. So William's influence lies in this city as well.

But today Lisieux is supremely devoted to St. Thérèse. One can visit Les Buissonnets, the picturesque house where she spent her childhood. Her body lies in a public chapel adjacent to the Carmelite convent she called home. There is also a beautiful basilica erected in her honor on a hill above the city.

Thérèse's vibrations are tangible in Lisieux. Laura and I enjoyed her sweet devotional quality, which seemed to mingle with the fragrance of summer flowers. On the other hand, it was strange to approach Lisieux the way we did. I think we would have felt more inspired if we had gone to Thérèse's town directly from Paris.

From my travel diary:

> Yogananda advised people not to compare saints since, as he put it, "The lives of great saints manifest in various ways the same, one God." (The New Path, p. ix) Nevertheless, in this instance I think it would be instructive to comment on the experience Laura and I had coming to Lisieux, immediately after immersing ourselves in William's sites.

Some who are familiar with history have doubts when they learn that Yogananda said he had been William the Conqueror in a past life. This isn't surprising, for William doesn't come off very well in many of the chronicles, ancient or modern. In fact, it takes some searching to unearth an English-language account of William's life that is in consonance with Yogananda's words. A cursory examination will give you no indication that William was a great soul.

And yet, Laura and I were fascinated to note that after our experiences in Caen, Dives, and Falaise, we felt a distinct spiritual-energy drop when we stayed in Lisieux: a town where people have consciously drawn on a saint's blessings for more than a century.

Now, don't get me wrong. Lisieux was wonderful. And Thérèse was a beautiful saint. We experienced a definite spiritual energy in the town. Thérèse's sweetness, her devotion to God, her divine love and compassion, permeate her childhood home, her convent, and the hilltop basilica that enthralled Catholics have erected in her honor.

But still, after we had been in Lisieux for a few hours, Laura and I missed the powerful, dynamic, life-transforming current of energy that had poured through us at the William sites. And we decided to cut our stay short, anxious to move on to other places connected with the Norman duke.

(In retrospect, Laura and I wondered whether some of the almost sleepy energy we experienced in Lisieux was caused by some of the pilgrims who had visited there. Perhaps they looked at Thérèse and imagined a sleepy peacefulness instead of the dynamic energy she had exerted to serve as a channel of love even while suffering a painful disease that took her life at an early age. Thérèse, we were sure, had been much more energetic than the feeling we experienced in her town.)

But, these reflections aside, I should emphasize again the beautiful spirit in the places made sacred by Thérèse—a spirit that grew, the longer we stayed in Lisieux. We recommend a visit there for any spiritual seeker traveling through Normandy.

Near Lisieux: The ruins of an old ducal castle, in use in William's day, stand in Fauguernon, about five miles northeast of Lisieux. It is likely that William stayed in this castle during his visits to the area.

You will have to take a back road to get there. On the map, it looks like pretty much of a straight drive. Ask around in Lisieux for the road to Fauguernon and its chateau. (With all the Catholic pilgrims, there are many English-speaking people in Lisieux.)

Here is Fauguernon's website:
http://tinyurl.com/37hygq

Click on Normandy, then click on Fauguernon, then click on the photo to see more views of the castle ruins.

Chapter 8

BEC

Bec (or L'Abbaye de Bec-Hellouin) is a hermitage founded by Hellouin, a medieval knight who became a monastic. It was here in 1042, a few years after it was founded, that the wandering monk Lanfranc showed up at the gates. And it was within these walls that William the Conqueror met Lanfranc, whom William would later accept as his spiritual guide, and who would, in William's words, be "entrusted with the care of his soul."

In the chapter of *Autobiography of a Yogi* titled "I Meet My Master, Sri Yukteswar," we read: "The obscuration of this life disappeared in a fragile dawn of prenatal memories. Dramatic time! Past, present, and future are its cycling scenes. This was not the first sun to find me at these holy feet!"

Circa 1050, in Bec, Normandy, one of the solar transits Yogananda referred to shone upon this earth.

SRI YUKTESWAR,
GURU OF PARAMHANSA YOGANANDA

To get to Bec from Lisieux, take N 13 east. After about twenty miles, turn left and go northeast onto N 138 – E 402. Then, after passing through Brionne, turn left again, going straight north on D 130. Within a few minutes, you should see signs for Bec. Follow them until you arrive at the small town of Bec-Hellouin, and steer into its tiny parking lot. From there, it's a five-minute walk to the old cloister. There is no admission charge.

Laura and I arrived at the monastery about midday. We were looking forward to experiencing William's vibrations, and especially those of the great saint, Sri Yukteswar, as Lanfranc.

As we entered the walls, our eyes were drawn to the dramatic tower that stands to the right of the main path. The fifteenth century structure is named after St. Nicholas, but it is also sometimes erroneously called Gundulf's Tower. (Gundulf was a monk of Bec—and contemporary of Lanfranc—who specialized in architecture. He designed the Tower of London for William after the conquest of England.)

Laura and I felt a deep peace. We wandered over to the ruins of the church where Hellouin and Lanfranc used to pray. Choosing seats on ancient stones, we sank into a reverie.

After a time, we got up to look for a place in the shade. A spot near to St. Nicolas's tower appealed to us. The energy felt even stronger than in the old church.

While meditating there, the image came to me of Sri Yukteswar teaching the boys in his seaside hermitage in Puri, India. In Bec, Lanfranc gained a similar reputation as an instructor of youth. In fact, he became famous through-

LAURA MEDITATING NEAR ST. NICOLAS'S TOWER

out France and all of Europe—kings and popes sent their young relatives to sit at his feet. One of Lanfranc's most famous pupils followed in his footsteps as Archbishop of Canterbury, Saint Anselm.

Lanfranc/Sri Yukteswar lived and taught here for years. The grounds are infused with his vibrations and blessings.

While Laura continued to meditate near St. Nicolas's tower, I went exploring. I walked Bec's sunlit paths and gazed at the monastery buildings. The trees, flowers, and singing birds whispered peace to my soul.

There is a clear division between the old and the relatively new on the grounds of this ancient monastery. There are the ruins of a medieval church, and a very old standing structure or two (including St. Nicolas's Tower), plus more recent buildings (built during the seventeenth and eighteenth centuries) obviously constructed long after Lanfranc lived here.

I discovered that the layout of the hermitage grounds was centered on a small brook that meandered past the walkways and under the new church. "Bec" is an old Viking word meaning "little stream." Here was the stream the monastery was named after.

I came back to find Laura still immersed in meditation. She had a deep experience in Bec. As she later wrote in her journal: "A blanket of peace descended and I lost interest in the external world. I tuned into Sri Yukteswar's consciousness and was keenly struck by how sweet it was. I was familiar with his reputation as an avatar of wisdom, but how sweet and loving he was. When Richard returned from his walk, my soul was soaring. Although it was very hot and humid, my spirit was refreshed. My soul had just been fed the sweetest nectar of divine joy. I will never forget my afternoon in Bec."

Unfortunately, we arrived when the buildings were closed, so we didn't see all that Bec had to offer. (The abbey is currently the home of Benedictine monks.) On the other hand, this was a blessing in disguise, as it forced us to turn our attentions inward–something which Lanfranc (the erstwhile hermit and monk) would have approved.

If you are interested in a guided tour of Bec Abbey, they are available from June through September on Mondays, Wednesdays, Thursdays, and Fridays at 10:30 AM, and 3, 4, and 5 PM, Saturdays at 10:30 AM and 3 and 4 PM, Sundays and holidays at noon and 3 and 4 PM; and, from October through May on Mondays and Wednesdays through Saturdays at 10:30 AM and 3 and 4 PM, Sundays and holidays at noon and 3 and 4 PM.

For more on the history of Bec, see:
www.newadvent.org/cathen/02379b.htm
www.france-for-visitors.com/normandy/le-bec-hellouin.html

Chapter 9

JUMIÈGES

If you have time, I recommend a quick visit to another medieval monastery, about forty minutes north of Bec. The Abbey of Jumièges doesn't have quite the same connections as Bec; however, it was one of the great monastic centers of William's day, and its abbot was a personal friend of William. The duke often visited here, and he was present when the church was consecrated in 1067.

From Bec, drive north on D 130, and turn right onto D 91. When you get to the town of Bourg-Achard, turn left onto D 313. After five or ten miles, you will see signs for Jumièges. Turn right where indicated and take the road down to the river. A ferry will take you and your vehicle across. Once on the other side, Jumièges is just a few minutes away.

I haven't found any listed hours for this site. As far as I know, it is always open for visitors.

JUMIÈGES ABBEY

Jumièges was founded by St. Philibert in 634. It reached its pinnacle of spiritual and secular influence in the eleventh century, when one of its prelates (Robert) became Archbishop of Canterbury. Over the centuries, it suffered from a number of political upheavals—the final one, the French Revolution, leaving it in its current condition.

The Abbey hosted an important scriptorium whose written works, including the historical chronicles of the celebrated William of Jumièges, are an important part of Normandy's medieval literary legacy.

Laura and I found Jumièges's tranquil grounds and ruined walls appealing. Time had altered its appearance, but a monastic serenity still lingered. Although it lacked the dynamic spiritual charge of Bec, we were glad we had come.

Jumièges is a popular tourist attraction. If you visit, be prepared for small crowds, children, etc. To meditate at the abbey, find a quiet spot behind a tree or a crumbling wall; but don't be surprised if you are interrupted.

Chapter 10

ROUEN

L ast but not least on our Normandy pilgrimage is the great city that stood as the base of operations for the dukes of Normandy during its several centuries as a separate power.

Rouen (pronounced "Rwah" by the locals) can be reached from Jumièges by taking the local service road north until you hit D 982. Turn right, and the highway will take you straight to Rouen. If you're coming from Bec, backtrack south a little ways on D 130. Then turn left onto N 138-E 402. When you reach the "Autoroute Normandie," turn right and follow the signs and roads northeast to downtown Rouen.

What's in Rouen? The ducal castle no longer stands, but . . . I'll let my travel diary tell the story:

Before coming to Normandy, I wrote to Swami Kriyananda (Yogananda's direct disciple) to tell him about our trip. In his response, Swamiji recommended that we seek out in Rouen a statue of William that looked like Yogananda. We didn't know where the statue stood, but figured it shouldn't be that hard to locate. While we were in Jumièges, a scholarly Frenchman directed us to where he thought the statue might be. And now a taxi dropped us off in the vicinity described by the scholar.

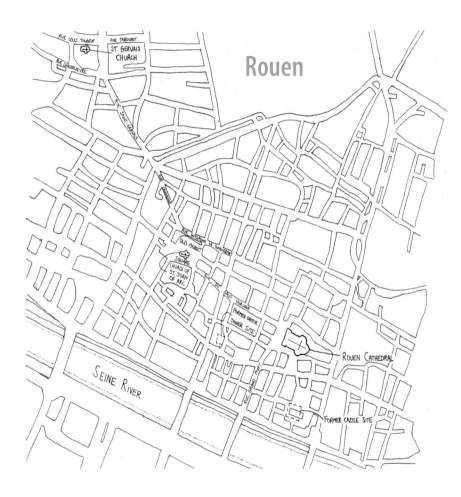

As we looked around, the first thing we saw was a dark and solemn church: St. Gervais. Laura and I inspected the building. Unfortunately, its doors were shut and no one seemed at home. (The St. Gervais church has limited hours. According to the Archdiocese of Rouen, it is only open for Mass every Sunday at 11 AM.)

ST. GERVAIS CHURCH

However, we received a reward for our efforts. On the northern wall was a plaque designating a historic site. It informed us that this was the spot where, in 1087, William the Conqueror had breathed his last. (Both William and his son Henry I died in Rouen.)

PLAQUE COMMEMORATING WILLIAM'S PASSING, ST. GERVAIS

We were elated. We had found the Norman version of the Biltmore Hotel! (Yogananda died in the Biltmore, in downtown Los Angeles, in 1952.)

Laura and I enjoyed for a time the energy surrounding the St. Gervais church, then continued our exploration of Rouen.

We continued walking downhill. Our next destination was the Vieux Marche–the old public square where, in 1431, Joan of Arc was put to death. We stopped at the spot where the event took place (marked by a sign surrounded by flower beds), then meditated in the rather unusual new church dedicated to St. Joan in the square. We both sensed a subtle light there.

Afterward, Laura and I explored the picturesque byways of the old section of Rouen. In the city's old cathedral (immortalized by Monet), we saw effigies on the tombs of William's ancestors, at least one of whom strongly resembled Yogananda (similar nose and mouth: see the William Longsword photo page 92).

The Rouen Cathedral was built in 1063, then destroyed by fire in 1200 and rebuilt. Only the left-hand spire remains from the original church that William would have visited. The cathedral is open Mondays from 2-6 PM, Tuesday through Saturday, from 7:45 AM to 7 PM, and on Sundays, from 8 AM to 6 PM. During winter it is open these same hours, except it closes from 12 to 2 PM, and after 6 PM. It is closed during Mass and on bank holidays.

(By the way, the Rouen Cathedral has a strong spiritual vibration. Laura and I felt it intensely during our second visit to Normandy, when we were fortunate to obtain a hotel room many stories up that faced the cathedral. When we opened our windows, the west wall of the church with its many saint statues stood about fifty yards away. They were in the process of cleaning the cathedral, so the statues were very bright, especially at night, shining in the darkness. We enjoyed the view very much, but had to shut our windows in the late hours, and not because of the temperature, which was warm. The energy emanating from the church was so strong that it prevented us from falling asleep.)

EFFIGY OF WILLIAM LONGSWORD,
WILLIAM THE CONQUEROR'S ANCESTOR,
ROUEN CATHEDRAL

At the end of a long day in Rouen (during my first visit), I lay in bed with my eyes closed, feeling Yogananda's presence. It struck me forcefully that William had claimed this city, too, as his own. Although it hadn't quite the personal color of Caen, his blessings were in Rouen as well.

The loving vibration felt like a farewell gift. This was our last evening in Normandy.

Also in Rouen: In William's day there was a large ducal castle in Rouen, nothing of which is left standing. (For the purposes of a William search, ignore Joan of Arc's Tower—Tour Jeanne D'Arc—near the Vieux Marche, part of a castle complex built more than a century after William's death.)

Two former castle locations are only a few minutes' walk from the Rouen Cathedral. They are located (1) on Rue C. St-Saens, and (2) between the Place de la Haute Vieille Tour and the Place de la Basse Vieille Tour (approximately where the Halle aux Toiles now stands). These former castle sites are marked on the Rouen map in this book.

Outside of Rouen: Near the town of Moulineaux, on the outskirts of Rouen, stands a ruined castle named after William's father (who was sometimes called "Robert the Devil"). Although the castle's name is perhaps apocryphal, the structure may have stood here in William's day, and if so, he would have been familiar with it.

Drive southwest through Rouen on N 338 (Voie Rapide Sud III), then take highway (autoroute) A13 west from the city.

You'll see the exit for Moulineaux after a few miles. The castle may even be visible from the highway, where it stands just south of it.

Rouen cathedral website:
www.sacred-destinations.com/france/rouen-cathedral

From Rouen, it's easy to hop a train back to Paris. It takes only an hour or two to get there.

Chapter 11

Off the Beaten Track: Other William Sites in Normandy

While researching this book, I didn't always find standing castles and churches in cities whose names loom large in William's history. Considering that we're focusing on events that took place nearly a thousand years ago, it's actually surprising that any structures remain. However, I imagine it may be possible to feel Yogananda's blessings in cities that no longer feature buildings that had stood in the Conqueror's day. If you visit these or other William sites not listed in this book, and experience his presence there, I would like to know.

Write to me at: info@CrystarPress.com.

I discovered a handful of William sites in Normandy (or nearby) that seemed to call for an extra effort to visit them. I'm adding them here, with a brief description and explanation.

Val-és-Dunes

It may surprise you that I'm listing this major William the Conqueror site, so near to Caen, so late in the book. The reasons are threefold:

First, I didn't visit this site either of the two times I went to Normandy, so I can't say what you might experience there.

Second, from all that I can see, except for a sign or two, there are no physical monuments to commemorate what happened in Val-és-Dunes. My impression is that peoples' experiences of this place consist of walking open fields. Now, this is true also of that very powerful site in Dives, yet my hesitation may make more sense when I mention that . . .

Third, Val-és-Dunes was a battlefield. Many people died there. William was deeply involved (see below), so you may feel inspiration. But battlefields can be intensely cathartic places for the spiritually sensitive—especially if it turns out you had left your body there! I myself have visited other battlefields, and even though I was glad I went, it was often difficult to feel inspiration. So I leave it to you to decide if you wish to visit. If you're not sure whether to go, you might meditate and see what guidance you receive, and then decide.

Now, let me explain why you might *want* to see Val-és-Dunes.

William had to climb a rocky path to claim his dukedom. His father died when he was about seven years old, and there were numerous attempts on his life by nobles who wished to wear the coronet. In 1047, those barons who were allied against

William's leadership gathered together, and William fought them at Val-és-Dunes. Showing his greatness at an early age (he was twenty), he defeated them with the help of his liege-lord, Henry I, king of France (who, later, fearing William's success, become the duke's enemy).

This battlefield marks the start of William's extraordinary career as a warrior. Until late in life, he never lost a battle. He was one of the greatest military leaders in history, and it all began in Val-és-Dunes.

Advertisements encourage visitors to participate in a guided tour out of the tourist office in nearby Argences. To get to Argences from Caen, drive southeast on D 613 for 10 kilometers. Turn left (north) at the D 40 motorway, and you should see the signs within a few minutes. The principal Val-és-Dunes battlefield appears to be located south of highway D 613, not far from Argences.

If you wish to stay overnight in the area, lodging is available. Check with the Argences tourist office.

For more information:
http://tinyurl.com/25z76w

Domfront

In this town lie the ruins of a castle that William besieged in 1049 and captured two years later. There are also several churches (Notre-Dame-sur-Eau and Saint-Symphorien) and an abbey (Lonlay) that date back to William's time.

Henry I also spent a considerable amount of time in Domfront, especially as a young man, and the town held a special place in his heart.

Domfront is located southwest of Falaise. It forms a triangle with Falaise to the northeast and Avranches (and Mont-Saint-Michel) to the northwest. If you decide to drive to Mont-Saint-Michel, you could swing through Domfront on your way to Falaise, if you don't mind taking smaller roads to get there. Use *Michelin* roadmaps to plot your route.

For more information on Domfront:

www.en.wikipedia.org/wiki/Château_de_Domfront

Fécamp

The ducal castle, centrally located in Fécamp next to the Abbey of the Holy Trinity, was the scene of William's triumphal return on Easter Sunday, 1067, from his conquest of England. The large hall hosted many knights and nobles for the celebratory banquet. From the photos, it appears that some walls and towers of the castle are still standing.

In addition, several of William's ancestors are entombed

next door in the abbey church, which is said to house the miraculous relic of Christ's blood. With their arguments, the Benedictines of Fécamp Abbey helped William make his case for invasion.

Fécamp is located on the Norman coast, northwest of Rouen. To drive to Fécamp from Rouen, take A 150 northwest out of the city, then turn left onto A 29-E 44. After about ten minutes, turn right onto D 926. It takes a few hours to arrive.

For more information, see:

http://freespace.virgin.net/doug.thompson/normandy/
fecamp.htm

http://tinyurl.com/yt7xq7

Arques-La-Bataille

In 1040, William the Conqueror's uncle, William of Arques, built a castle that overlooks the town of Arques-La-Bataille, just four miles southeast of Dieppe. William felt uneasy about his uncle and this castle, so he took it over. The castle's foundations and some walls still stand. Call ahead before you go: sometimes the fortress is closed for reconstruction. However, even at those times, you can still visit and enjoy it from a distance.

Trains run through Arques. You should be able to reach it from Rouen's station (Rouen Rive Droit). Be sure to check beforehand; if you take a train for Dieppe, it may be a nonstop commuter train. (When I tried booking a rail pass online from

Rouen to Arques using Rail Europe, the destination listed was Dieppe Ville.) You want to make sure your train will stop in Arques; if not, you may need to take a bus or taxi back to Arques from Dieppe.

To drive to Arques-La-Bataille from Rouen, head north on A 150. Take the A 151 exit, going north. At some point during your drive, A 151 will become N 27. Before you reach Dieppe, turn right (east) onto D 54. From there, it's only about three miles to Arques-La-Bataille.

Eu

In 1050, William married Matilda of Flanders in this city. The marriage took place in the chapel of the castle. I have read conflicting reports—that the chapel is the only part of the original castle still standing, and that nothing remains of the original castle (destroyed in 1475). I am still researching this question.

Whether the chapel remains, however, it is clear that the current Chateau D'Eu stands on the location of the old Castle of Augi, where William and Matilda celebrated their nuptials. Sections of the Chateau D'Eu are open for tourists. Check the websites listed below for castle hours and other information.

For the Eu train situation, see the St. Valery-sur-Somme description below.

To drive to Eu from Rouen, take A 28-E 402, northwest out of the city. Turn left or northeast onto D 49.

For more information, see:
http://tinyurl.com/3b2w7f, http://tinyurl.com/3ymvkp

St.-Valery-sur-Somme

After William and his invasion force had waited at Dives-sur-Mer for six weeks, the wind finally changed direction and they started sailing toward England. The weather became stormy and they had to turn back, traveling northeast along the coast. A few of the ships capsized and some men were lost. The fleet took sanctuary in the bay of St.-Valery-sur-Somme, and William took advantage of the local history to re-inspire his discouraged men.

Before he died in 632, Saint Valery asked that his bones be buried at this location. William went to the funeral chapel and disinterred the saint's body. Saint Valery was known for miraculously protecting sailors. The men prayed to the saint and felt his inspiration. Under William's urging, they asked the saint to shift the wind once more. Within a few hours, the wind shifted direction, and the invasion took place—with extraordinary and historic results.

The saint's chapel (Chapel of the Sailors) still stands in St.-Valery-sur-Somme. There are also "Guillaume Towers" and a "Guillaume door" nearby, but I haven't been able to find any information about them. Like Bayeux, St.-Valery is a well-preserved medieval town with a Gothic church. I wouldn't be surprised if pilgrims going there would experience William's presence in various parts of the city, and especially near the coast.

Railroad tracks lead into St.-Valery from higher up the Somme Valley. But it isn't clear whether that line carries passenger trains. I see no Rail France line heading into St.-Valery. You may have to go by bus or car. Check with a travel agent.

To drive to St.-Valery-sur-Somme from Rouen, simply go northeast on A 28-E 402. It will take several hours to arrive.

Note: Fécamp, Arques-La-Bataille, Eu, and St.-Valery-sur-Somme are all located north of Rouen, on or near the Normandy coast. If these sites interest you, you may wish to plan a trip that encompasses all of them—by driving first to either Fécamp or St.-Valery-sur-Somme, then going northeast (from Fecamp) or southwest (from St.-Valery-sur-Somme) along the coast, stopping at each site along the way until you reach the last destination, then returning to Rouen. (Route D 925 will take you from Fécamp to Dieppe—just north of Arques-La-Bataille—then to Eu. From Eu, take D 940 to St.-Valery-sur-Somme.) This trip will likely take several days, so I would recommend reserving a hotel room in one of the middle cities (Arques or Eu).

A Countryside of Churches

William and his followers and their offspring were big on church building. In his book, *A Place in Normandy*, Nicholas

Kilmer wrote: "the Conqueror's family [blanketed Normandy] with what historians call a 'white mask of churches.'" (pp. 103-104)

You will find these ancient chapels dotting the hillsides. Although some have been lost over time, quite a few remain. Drive through the Norman countryside and you're likely to see one.

It is said that William never missed Mass in his life. Since he traveled widely throughout his domains, if you locate a church that's old enough, it's quite possible that William worshipped there.

Similarly with old Norman castles. Whether or not there is any record of William's connection with a place, if it existed in his day, it's likely that he stopped by at least for a visit.

In addition, it's unlikely that every preserved William anecdote has made its way into history books or onto the Internet. Some stories may be preserved by the locals. If you stop at an old church or castle, inquire as to whether "Guillaume le Conquérant" ever came there. You may hear an interesting story. (If so, I'd like to hear it, too!)

I've listed below a wonderful website on Norman churches and castles. It can be helpful if you are driving through Normandy and want to know if there is anything of interest in the area. Check the towns you will pass through, then click their names if they show up on this web page.

Please note: Some of the buildings listed went up long after William and Lanfranc. Look for structures that were built in the eleventh century and earlier.

Also: this is another of those translated web pages. It may take some time to work out what the words mean. Be aware that some town names may have been translated into English (e.g. "Falaise" into "Cliff").

Anyway, here's the site. Happy hunting!

http://tinyurl.com/37hygq

Click first on Normandy, then click on the town you wish to investigate.

Other helpful web sites:

General Normandy travel website:

www.visitnormandy.org/Normandy.nsf

Rail France map:

www.raileurope.com/europe-travel-guide/france/map.html

Chapter 12

THE TWELFTH KRIYA

W ere *you* with William? Many who feel a connection with
Yogananda probably were. Perhaps a trip to Normandy will
answer the question. But that is not the only reason to go.

Each of a spiritual master's incarnations has a unique flavor.
William's lifetime was highly active and visible. His actions
changed the world. He held a position of authority and leadership, he played a large role on the world's stage, and he
channeled divine power and will through everything he did.

Lifetimes pass like waves, washing over the sands of centuries. Through the ever-changing backdrop of places, people,
and languages, one constant remains—God pursues us, bearing
his message of love and redemption.

William, that great leader of souls, came again as Paramhansa
Yogananda to lead us in the conquest of delusion. He has
placed in our hands the "weapons" of techniques, teachings,
and grace. If we would only make the effort, we too can
claim as our own the Kingdom across the sea.

May Yogananda walk with you.

P.S. Dear reader, if you discover other details about William or his sites during your Normandy trip, and would like to share them with others, please send me the information at info@ CrystarPress.com and I will include it in future editions of this book, with acknowledgements and thanks.

About the Author

Richard Salva was born in Cleveland, Ohio. While in his teens, he became interested in yoga philosophy and reincarnation. He obtained his first job in order to visit a yoga community in California called Ananda. (Ananda follows the teachings of Paramhansa Yogananda, author of the spiritual classic, *Autobiography of a Yogi*. Ananda was founded by Yogananda's direct disciple, Swami Kriyananda.) Two years later, Richard moved to Ananda Village. He has been part of Ananda ever since, and incorporates thirty-five years of meditation, and study and practice of the deeper teachings of yoga, into his writings.

For five years, Richard lived as a monk in the yoga community's monastery. He began to give sermons and lectures, and was ordained as a minister. He was sent out to help start budding communities in Northern California and Italy. He continued to teach classes in the United States and in Europe, and began to allude to his historical studies in his talks.

About fifteen years ago, Richard began an in-depth study based on Paramhansa Yogananda's statement that he (Yogananda) was William the Conqueror in a past life, and that Yogananda's guru, Swami Sri Yukteswar, had been William's priest and advisor, Lanfranc. He also researched Swami Kriyananda's belief that he (Swami) had been William's son, Henry I—and found much evidence to support all of these connections.

Richard developed and co-taught classes based on these subjects, and in the early 2000s traveled twice with his wife to Normandy to visit sites made famous by William, Lanfranc, and Henry I.

Richard is also the author of *The Reincarnation of Abraham Lincoln*, a critically acclaimed title based on another statement by Yogananda.

At present, Richard continues to write books on subjects related to Yogananda's teachings. He lives, with his wife and son (named William, after the Conqueror), near Ananda Village in Nevada City, California.

Richard plans to lead pilgrimages to William the Conqueror sites in Normandy and England. If you are interested in taking part in such a pilgrimage, and would like more information, contact Richard at info@CrystarPress.com.

FURTHER EXPLORATIONS

If you would like to learn more about Paramhansa Yogananda and his teachings, or about Swami Kriyananda, Crystal Clarity Publishers offers many additional resources to assist you.

Crystal Clarity publishes the original 1946, unedited edition of Paramhansa Yogananda's spiritual masterpiece

 ## Autobiography of a Yogi
Paramhansa Yogananda

Autobiography of a Yogi is one of the best-selling Eastern philosophy titles of all time, with millions of copies sold, named one of the best and most influential books of the twentieth century. This highly prized reprinting of the original 1946 edition is the only one available free from textual changes made after Yogananda's death. Yogananda was the first yoga master of India whose mission was to live and teach in the West.

In this updated edition are bonus materials, including a last chapter that Yogananda wrote in 1951, without posthumous changes. This new edition also includes the eulogy that Yogananda wrote for Gandhi, and a new foreword and afterword by Swami Kriyananda, one of Yogananda's close, direct disciples.

The New Path
My Life with Paramhansa Yogananda
Swami Kriyananda

The New Path tells the story of a young American's spiritual quest, his discovery of the powerful classic, *Autobiography of a Yogi*, and his subsequent meeting with—and acceptance as a disciple by—the book's author, the great spiritual teacher and yoga master, Paramhansa Yogananda.

The New Path provides a marvelous sequel to Paramhansa Yogananda's own *Autobiography of a Yogi*, helping you to gain a more profound understanding of this great world teacher. Through hundreds of stories of life with Yogananda and through Swami Kriyananda's invaluable insights, you'll discover the inner path that leads to soul-freedom and lasting happiness.

Praise for *The New Path*

"Reading Autobiography of a Yogi *by Yogananda was a transformative experience for me and for millions of others. In* The New Path, *Kriyananda carries on this great tradition. Highly recommended."*
  –Dean Ornish, M.D., Founder and President, Preventative Medicine Research Institute, Clinical Professor of Medicine, University of California, San Francisco, author, *The Spectrum*

"Not only did Kriyananda walk in the footsteps of an enlightened master, The New Path *makes it obvious that he himself became an embodiment of Yogananda's teachings."*
  –Michael Bernard Beckwith, featured contributor to The Secret, author, *Spiritual Liberation–Fulfilling Your Soul's Potential*

Two Souls: Four Lives
The Lives and Former Lives of
Paramhansa Yogananda
and his disciple, Swami Kriyananda
Catherine Kairavi

This book explores an astonishing statement made by Paramhansa Yogananda, that he was the historical figure, William the Conqueror, in a previous incarnation.

The Norman Conquest of England was one of the pivotal moments in world history, a series of events that affects us even today. Is it possible that two of the greatest men of that era—William the Conqueror and his son, Henry I of England—have recently reincarnated as the great spiritual master Paramhansa Yogananda (author of the classic *Autobiography of a Yogi*) and his close disciple, Swami Kriyananda? If so, what are the subtle connections between the Norman Conquest and modern times?

Praise for *Two Souls: Four Lives*

"[This book] is a fascinating journey through time. . . . In acknowledging that the souls of Paramhansa Yogananda and Norman King William the Conqueror, and his son Henry and Yogananda's disciple Swami Kriyananada, may indeed be the same, readers may shift their view of both politics and spirituality. [It] tantalizes your intellect, stirs your soul, and challenges you to relook at your current, even multiple-life missions."
   –Barbara Lane, PhD, author of *16 Clues to Your Past Lives, Echoes from the Battlefield*, and *Echoes from Medieval Halls*

"Two Souls: Four Lives *is well-researched, authoritative and totally convincing. Kairavi has done a valuable service for anyone interested in reincarnation, history or spiritual growth. The books of Paramhansa Yogananda and Swami Kriyananda are modern-day classics. I'm convinced this book will become a classic, too."*
   –Richard Webster, author of *Soul Mates* and *Practical Guide to Past-Life Memories*

Finalist for New Age Nonfiction—Best Books 2006 Book Awards

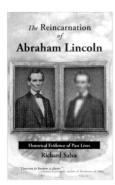

The Reincarnation of Abraham Lincoln
Historical Evidence of Past Lives
Richard Salva

Is it possible President Lincoln returned to twentieth century America. . . and we didn't recognize him? Based on the words of the great world teacher, Paramhansa Yogananda, *The Reincarnation of Abraham Lincoln* presents nearly five hundred fascinating similarities in the personalities, characters, and life circumstances of Abraham Lincoln and Charles Lindbergh.

The astonishing Lincoln-Lindbergh connections span every aspect of human expression and experience—from the physical to the mental, emotional, social, and spiritual. Parallel stories from the lives of both men demonstrate how the hidden laws of karma and reincarnation impact our daily lives.

Praise for *The Reincarnation of Abraham Lincoln*

"★★★★★"–FOREWORD CLARION REVIEWS

"★★★★★"–MIDWEST BOOK REVIEW

"A+!"–DR. ROBERT HIERONIMUS, host of 21st Century Radio, author of *Founding Fathers, Secret Societies*

"One unstoppable read of reincarnation." –SOMA B. DAS, Hinduism.about.com

A compelling case study. . . . [goes] far beyond the realm of coincidence or superficial likeness." –LIGHT OF CONSCIOUSNESS Magazine

Accepted into the Abraham Lincoln Presidential Library

Karma and Reincarnation
The Wisdom of Yogananda, Volume 2
Paramhansa Yogananda

Many people share theories on reincarnation, or karma, or what happens at death. Yogananda, a master of yoga, writes from his own true knowledge and experience. Coming through Yogananda's words, above all, is the deepest encouragement to every reader: the reassurance that God loves us, and that all of life is designed to help us move toward our own highest fulfillment.

Topics included: Why do we see a world of suffering and inequality? How should we handle the challenges in our lives? What happens at death, and after death? Is there a heaven? What is the origin and purpose of reincarnation? This book offers fascinating answers for life's great mysteries, but, more importantly, it tells you how to make the most of every day of the life you've been given.

As Yogananda explains the operation of karma, death, and reincarnation, he also shares the deeper purpose of existence for every soul. Understanding these truths can bring clarity, confidence, and inspiration into your life.

Crystal Clarity Publishers presents *The Wisdom of Yogananda* series features writings of Paramhansa Yogananda not available elsewhere. These books capture the Master's expansive and compassionate wisdom, his sense of fun, and his practical spiritual guidance. The titles include writings from his earliest years in America, in an approachable, easy-to-read format. The words of the Master are presented with minimal editing, to capture the fresh and original voice of one of the most highly regarded spiritual teachers of the twentieth century.

CRYSTAL CLARITY PUBLISHERS

When you're seeking a book on practical spiritual living, you want to know it's based on an authentic tradition of timeless teachings, and that it resonates with integrity. This is the goal of Crystal Clarity Publishers: to offer you books of practical wisdom filled with true spiritual principles that have not only been tested through the ages, but also through personal experience.

We publish only books that combine creative thinking, universal principles, and a timeless message. Crystal Clarity books will open doors to help you discover more fulfillment and joy by living and acting from the center of peace within you.

Crystal Clarity Publishers—recognized worldwide for its best-selling, original, unaltered edition of Paramhansa Yogananda's classic *Autobiography of a Yogi*—offers many additional resources to assist you in your spiritual journey, including over ninety books, a wide variety of inspirational and relaxation music composed by Swami Kriyananda, Yogananda's direct disciple, and yoga and meditation DVDs.

For our online catalog, complete with secure ordering, please visit us on the web at: **www.crystalclarity.com**

We offer many of our book titles in unabridged MP3 format audiobooks. To purchase these titles and to see more music and audiobook offerings, visit our website www.crystalclarity.com. Or look for us in many of the popular online download sites.

To request a catalog, place an order for the products you read about in the *Further Explorations* section of this book, or to find out more information about us and our products, please contact us:

CONTACT INFORMATION

14618 Tyler Foote Rd. • Nevada City, CA 95959

phone: 800-424-1055 or 530-478-7600

online: www.crystalclarity.com

email: clarity@crystalclarity.com

ANANDA SANGHA WORLDWIDE

Ananda Sangha is a fellowship of kindred souls following the teachings of Paramhansa Yogananda. The Sangha embraces the search for higher consciousness through the practice of meditation, and through the ideal of service to others in their quest for Self-realization. Approximately ten thousand spiritual seekers are affiliated with Ananda Sangha throughout the world.

Founded in 1968 by Swami Kriyananda, a direct disciple of Paramhansa Yogananda, Ananda includes seven communities in the United States, Europe, and in India. Worldwide, about one thousand devotees live in these spiritual communities, which are based on Yogananda's ideals of "plain living and high thinking."

"Thousands of youths must go north, south, east and west to cover the earth with little colonies, demonstrating that simplicity of living plus high thinking lead to the greatest happiness!" After pronouncing these words at a garden party in Beverly Hills, California in 1949, Paramhansa Yogananda raised his arms, and chanting the sacred cosmic vibration AUM, "registered in the ether" his blessings on what has become the spiritual communities movement. From that moment on, Swami Kriyananda dedicated himself to bringing this vision from inspiration to reali-

118

ty by establishing communities where home, job, school, worship, family, friends, and recreation could evolve together as part of the interwoven fabric of harmonious, balanced living. Yogananda predicted that these communities would "spread like wildfire," becoming the model lifestyle for the coming millennium.

Swami Kriyananda lived with his guru during the last four years of the Master's life, and continued to serve his organization for another ten years, bringing the teachings of Kriya Yoga and Self-realization to audiences in the United States, Europe, Australia, and, from 1958–1962, India. In 1968, together with a small group of close friends and students, he founded the first "world-brotherhood community" in the foothills of the Sierra Nevada Mountains in northeastern California. Initially a meditation retreat located on sixty-seven acres of forested land, Ananda World Brotherhood Village today encompasses one thousand acres where about 250 people live a dynamic, fulfilling life based on the principles and practices of spiritual, mental, and physical development, cooperation, respect, and divine friendship.

After forty years of existence, Ananda is one of the most successful networks of intentional communities in the world. Urban communities have been developed in Palo Alto and Sacramento, California; Portland, Oregon; and Seattle, Washington. In Europe, near Assisi, Italy, a spiritual retreat and community was established in 1983, where today nearly one hundred residents from eight countries live. In Pune and Gurgaon, India there are two communities and a spiritual retreat center.

Ananda Sangha Worldwide contact information (see following page).

Contact Information

Ananda Sangha Worldwide
14618 Tyler Foote Rd. • Nevada City, CA 95959
phone: 530-478-7560
online: www.ananda.org
email: sanghainfo@ananda.org

Expanding Light Retreat
14618 Tyler Foote Rd. • Nevada City, CA 95959
phone: 800-346-5350
online: www.expandinglight.org
email: info@expandinglight.org